The Marmalade Kid

by Ian Phillips

The Marmalade Kid

by Ian Phillips

Shame and Blame

It's a shame
that we name and
feel the need to blame
when we are all the same
in this game

We brush our teeth
Clean our words
So the next ones mean more
Gleam. Make you notice
Coz if you're clean inside
You feel no shame

One pay check away from Blame.
And Shame. And Pain and
No job. And no Colgate.
Where politics dissolve
With healthy resolve.

The Huddle

It's 10. am and the laughter's loud
and beer is on the breath.
A huddle of four putting world to rights
and fighting to the death.
One's on Tinder smirking and waiting for a bite.
The other's painting pictures,
of another building site.

Their weapon of wit a repertoire,
where every girl's a catch.
They throw loose words with hard intent
then reach down for a scratch.
Comments made she hears them,
and throws back uneasy smiles,
And the roars of appreciation
echoed on for miles.

My Uncle Lies Here

My uncle lies here
in this meadowed land
under bushes and hidden from view.
A Cross marks the place
where his ashes were cast
in the summer of '72.

I recall that kind words were spoken
When like snow he floated to ground
And that Emily gripped
my hand in anger
his dark secrets
ne'er to be found.

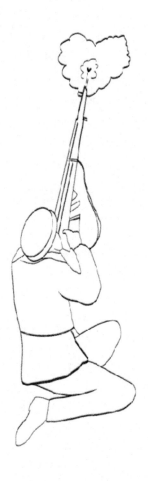

Aiming High

I'm aiming high amongst this world
Of rampant choice and fate.
I'm loading my gun
and I'm setting a date
Watching mountains above
over valleys of hate.

I'm brewing up some tea
now my target's in plain sight.
Though there's cramping in my thigh
 and there's a fading of the light.
It's the reasons of my choices past
 and a will before the fight.
But I'm aiming high you see
because I know deep down
what's ultimately right.

Rebirth by Nia Phillips

Staring out at a great expanse,

a space so wide,

you wish to be swallowed up whole by it,

comforted by the soft soil tumbling on your skin like old coffee grind,

layering a delicate weight on your body; a weighted blanket from nature,

sealing off the noise, the distraction,

replaced by deafening silence.

Finally, your mouth filled with soil,

you can breathe.

Getting Through

We'll get through this, Chris she said
As she pummelled pillows
and sized up his head.
But you need to change and listen more
As she subconsciously watched him
and kicked him to the floor.

I love you Julie, Chris said back
but you're asking me to change.
And the power of undoing is not easy to arrange.
The story of Us is entwined high above.
Ingredients measured
with large scoops of love.

And Julie was nodding as she
smoothed down the bed.
She was thinking of his bald patch
 and the state of his shed.
She thought of the children
and the blessings that they bring
And she thought of him laughing
When she first made him king.

Fourteen years later and the kids have all fled.
And it's Jim that she's Tindered with
and laying in his bed.
Chris lives up in Norwich where
 he sails with all the broads.
And on long, cold nights they text each other
Like two pensioned, loving frauds.

Sometimes

Sometimes I feel you
slipping through my fingers.
Like a fading morning dream,
Splitting at the seams.
Around you I feel I have
the presence of a ghost.
A sea without a coast.
A companion at most.

Flushing away these thoughts
 like disinfectant down a drain.
Your strength of love for me is clear,
 you're the bandage on my sprain.
Drifting to each other like leaves
falling from two trees.
You're the dolphin in my bath water
and you bring me to me knees.

So Far and yet so Near.

Parts of me lay tethered
to docks I never see,
Through blackened clouds
I'm reaching out
For a lock without a key.

I'm the statue in Trafalgar Square
 unsure of your return.
I'm the book you haven't read yet
On a shelf you want to burn.

We may not be each other
but my finish is your start.
The kite line is still tethered
as a beat is to a heart.
As you push on forwards facing,
Waves that breach your sea.
Draw your strength from where you came
and who you want to be.

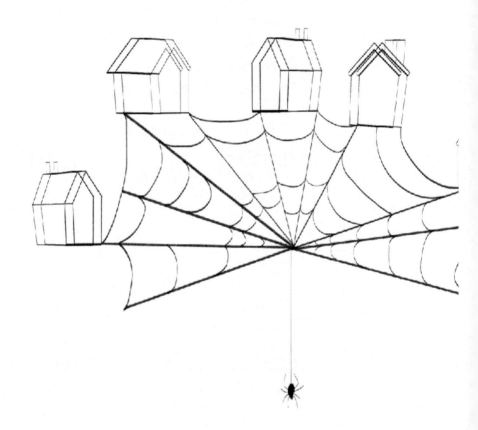

Little Houses

She's got them all laid out her houses
all in a little row.
She knows what's what and who she is and
she's white as driven snow.
She knows everything from nothing but
god protect her source.
With a smile she'll say how dare you ask
As you stand outside her cause.

And behind her eyes lies sadness like
a web of dark decay.
They said she had no loving like
a potter low on clay.
But beware these men and women who
draw you to their lair
And spit you out like tasteless gum
with an understanding glare.

The Tourist Boat

The tourist boats set sail again
half-crammed on upper deck.
While partners grip each others arms
with thin smiles kept in check.

Masks flap on wrists like bracelets
bristling in the breeze
And the muffled screams of children
hang like nightmares on the seas.

Emotions melt like ice-creams
as they scupper onto land.
While the sun exposes lovers and
a tan-less wedding band.

And seagulls screech their greetings in
blue skies overhead
And mums read stories of better times
to children in their bed.

The Marmalade Kid

I'm blinded by the raging sun,
glaring through the clouds.
I'm reaching out for falling chords
imprinted on your shroud.
This wave is breaking over me,
my senses overcome,
Then Jessie lays her hand on me
and I turn to face the drum.

She wraps her cloak around me
and leads me to the chair.
She sings to me her life story
 from a world that didn't care.
And in her voice is beauty and
music's healing balm

And a sense that she will always be,
a lake of cool and calm.

The Balloon

Love sits mostly
like an invisible balloon
Amongst families
nudged, leant against
Mostly ignored

Every now and then
it is recognised
And it inflates slightly
Buoyed by the attention
Before Settling

As we lean across
This balloon, to point
And shout and misunderstand
it takes our weight
Without complaint.

I see the balloon,
Sometimes know it is there
And try to make room for it
As it selflessly waits
Linking our hands

Drawing a Line

I draw a line and I ask for the bill.
I ask the clocks to stop
and that the rivers be still.
My age remains timeless,
I am as I was.
Entering the stage
to a loving applause.

The sun shines down brightly,
freezing my time
All that I know stands,
before me in a line.
And nothing is there, that I would
not love or know.
Each one is a part of me,
engaged in my flow.

Mother time clicks her fingers
and onward we go.
And my train leaves the station,
 my past no longer the show.
Not knowing the future,
nor where arrows will fall,
Resolute that I am part of this,
until the curtains call.

A Calm

Quiet your busy mind my child.
Push all your fears away.
Put up the ramparts and raise the bridge
And let the angels have their say.

Wrap up warm and face the wind,
Embrace the freshness that it brings.
And when it tires as it always will,
Hear the silence as it sings.

All things will pass as nature shows,
Like thunderstorms inside the mind.
Calm your busy thoughts my child,
And feel your loving soul unwind.

White Dog

Feeling morning sunshine,
warm a waking face. Watching stretching trees
affirm their silent grace.
Stepping onto grass that's burning morning's dew.
Forgotten footballs waiting,
in grass that's overdue.

It's the killer in the distance,
it's that calm before the storm.
Where anger's close to boiling
and the kettle's only warm.
Sharpened words and whitened
knuckles reaching for the door,
Into a dark confinement that
drags my heart along the floor.

Breaking waves of mint I sense
crushed underneath my shoe.
And god is there still preaching
to an empty jasmined pew. Distant bells are chiming
for an audience never seen,
And roses hide their secret scent
for the bees without a queen.
Everything is there to show me,
like a sleeping dog at rest.
Like an empty chair just waiting,
or a swallow's empty nest.
Answers that I am seeking sit
like holy water never blessed,
Dormant barely visible, a sin not yet confessed.

The Lighthouse

If the ship in which you're sailing,
blows into a stormy sea.
And the gale-force winds around you
ignore your desperate plea.
Hold on tight throughout this madness
because everything will pass,
And somewhere in the darkness burns
a flame to guide your mast.

Don't become that sunken shipwreck,
laying in a watered grave.
Seek out the guiding light
and your wounded heart she'll save.
The lighthouse beam of goodness
hidden deep within our bones,
Will land your soul forever
on a beach of polished stones.

The Voices

It's the voices, they tell me,
that are sending me insane
That explain the level playing fields
 and show me who's to blame
It's the voices, that stop me,
from punching you in the face,
When you smile at me, spit guile at me,
remind me of my place.

It's the voices that explain to me,
when to cross the road.
To take heed of red and green
and don't be one to goad.
It's the voices, advising me,
as hatred gushes from your hole,
the stench of your embittered spirit,
the darkness of your soul.

It's the voices that advise me,
pay your bills and play the game
Work hard and play hard my friend,
your breakdown is my aim.
It's the voices that will tell me,
just where my head is at
and the revenge that boils
within me means my prayers are falling flat.

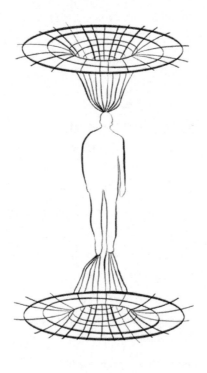

I always want more

I always want more
I want a space between now
and the ending
I want pauses before the credits
to absorb what I have seen
I want extra time
before the final whistle blows
I don't want the bill,
I want the starter again
I want to be handed the menu.
I want my choices again.
I want to keep the engine running
as my destination approaches,
I don't want the song to complete
it's final fading chords,
I don't want to turn that final page
And feel words concluding, ending
before turning to white.

Polo Day

The green lawn of carpet
The sculptured beasts of hell
Riders thundering towards us
Lowly mensen.
Behind fences I sip champagne
And contemplate,
My country's future leaders.

Gnarled Beauty

It's a gnarled beauty
that you are showing
Its roots fucked and
clearly not growing.
Do you water yourself
with piss?
Am I that easy to dismiss?

Your words are coated
in venom
And I can envisage
your double-denim
I'm not Carol and you've
not got a friend
remember that when you
meet your bitter end.

Your Time is Up

I'm losing patience with this world.

And I'm making a plan.

To live in a van.

To cook when I can

And I'll sift golden rivers with

someone called Stan.

And if I may be blunt

My friendships require a shunt

Your views are too nice

and my heads in a vice

And I've no time for Steinbeck's mice.

So listen up because this is me.

And my time is short and never free.

Your care-home acceptance

of what's good and bad

is lazy and life-less and

makes you look sad.

So walk on by and unhook yourself

from me.

Your time is up,

you can hand back my key.

Do Cows Spoon in the Dark?

Driving fast,

past blurs of black,

brown and white Splats,

I wonder if cows crave Prozac?

No anoraks, wellies,

small umbrellas.

Just a stare ahead

and sometimes to one side.

An occasional chew and down it comes,

Vertical rain bouncing

on moccasin bare backs,

Streaming down

venisonal fragile, bent bones.

Far off mooing oft mistaken for groans

Alone in the black,

a touch on the knee,

Do scared cows spoon

when no ones there to see?

Nibbling small ears clamped

with cardboard tags.Forgetting for now

how their belly sags

Red horror dreams, the futures not far.

Love's final promise,

the Abattoir .

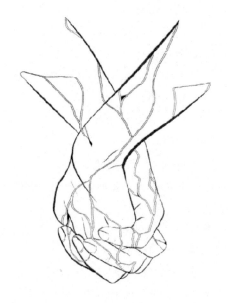

So we decided to stay together

So we decided to stay together
Not cry and part and regret
Our roads remained conjoined
Not parting towards separate sunsets
We glued that which was broke
Instead of settling debts and gently
handing back keys.
We dived out of the eye of the storm
At first swirling, hands gripping hands
And landed bruised, hurt, damaged
Yet together.

Red

I like red, not the colour but the word.

I like the word that rhymes with read

And dead, and bed.

I like red as it hides within blood

And its skies at night,

when red, delights men in fields.

I like red for flying the flag

And standing tall

And for staining roses

And bloodied noses.

A day off

As you lie, waiting

for a final breath.

Recall that blue-skied day,

When the cool morning sun

Promised fresh river breezes

And oars dipped into honey.

If you have one regret

Don't make it that on that glistening day

Work called out and gripped your soul.

The Origin of My Species

When I die it will be the start

of something

A start of the fading

memory of me.

An evaporation of our love

That we carried together and

then there was just me.

It will be the start of our children

Untying the boat and

pushing us out to sea.

The start of occasional sadness

for friends whom we

Can no longer reach

Of repainting walls in

our once loved house.

Of pausing over photographs,

smiling, smiling.

And while I know lights

will be turned off

the origin of my death

will be marked,

by that deep resonance

within my children's soul.

What is....

What is your memory of me?
When I was delivered in front of you
That force that had scooped me up
And like a quivering arrow,
I landed at your feet.

What is your memory of me?
As my shy drunken eyes
Shone in anticipation.
And our histories remained secret,
Intimacy at the forefront.

What is your memory of me?
As we laugh at our now shared lives.
At our realised unplanned dreams.
At our diluted selves within our children.
At the fears that await us now,
And still your hand feels small in mine.

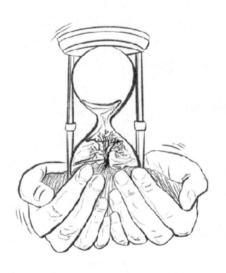

Each morning..

Each morning I brush my teeth
And stare in the mirror
And remember I am over forty
So cancer fills my mind.

Each morning I reach for slippers
That I haven't bought yet
And rub my back that holds no aches
Yet before long, shall.

Each morning I think
About when I will not be here
And when the theatre curtains draw
Will the exit sign still be burning?

Each morning I awake and smile
And hope for a day of blue skies
Of unplanned laughter
Of days without mourning.

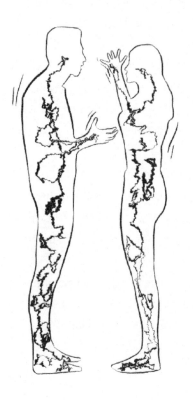

Conversing deflections

Your words bounce off my skin
Grazing, scratching, hurting.
I feel for my weapon
And carefully load in reply.
It's another Valentine's Day slaughter.

You absorb all I fire at you
And there are no exit wounds.
Just another part of you,
Accepting what I am.

This be The Verve...

They sort you out, your mum and dad

Instil you with goodness and ideas

And love.

And they were sorted and loved

By their parents too

In swirling skirts, tanned faces

Fifties, techicolor photographs.

Like a glorious virus we pass on

Our happiness and hope to man.

Revelling, lying in this warm sweet honey,

conjoined by timeless laughter.

Original "This Be The Verse" by Philip Larkin

Valerie's getting Old

She's getting old, that Valerie, they said.

Had all her bits pulled up not long back

Now bronchitis is eating her up

It'll just take one thing,

then she'll be gone.

This badge of oldness she wears

so forlornly, as she shuffles

staring at her mortal coil.

And then the pause,

The recognition of cool breath

on her warmed skin

The glow of sun through closed eyes

That returns her to

the calmness of womb.

Everyone Should See This Bed

Everyone should see this bed

Where hope falters and

Heroes are welcomed

And praised

That right was done.

Where hands are held

And memories are hurriedly

Remembered

When all he wants to do

Is look forward

Not back.

Where the whiteness of sheets

Almost promise to heal

And all that intensity of love

In one room

Is known to fail.

Closet racists

Closet racists wait and only come out
When their word's safety holds no doubt.
Soapy poison bubbles floating around,
Opinion clouded, above the ground
I don't see you as black they confess
And yet choosing the orange for the ripeness,
The pith, the juice, peel, pips, I express
Sorrow at such, sudden, utter colour blindness.

On match days miracles are cardinal.
Amongst veins of stench in the urinal,
Deformed strangers talk cheap disturbing news,
Where it's easy to tell the reds from the blues.
And as floodlights dim the blacks from the whites,
Soon scarves will hang like discarded kites.

Innocent Horizons

Lying in that innocent grass
Sun in one eye, so you squint.
So close to the ground, you count the blades.
It was so innocent,

you could pick a blade and taste the day.
Only size 4 and below are allowed,
those who only know the

boundaries of this sweet land

and nothing else.
Bounded by trees with tempting gaps.
Gaps that tempt the smokers and

innocent lovers who know nothing.

Looking across the lop-sided land

through one eye,
at the white goal posts with no nets.
Realising that there was nothing to stop your goals.

And on those sweet playing fields,
where we practiced Life's games,
nothing is apparent.
Only that the grass stains don't matter yet

and that soon the whistle will be heard

Tales From The Riverbank

Bad memories fade fast.

Only bitterness remains for those who demand
on pocketing images that we should know

Are worthless.

Those strong summer days

Stretching out amongst immature limbs.
And as you lay, close up to that blade of grass,
unknowingly placing a perspective on Life

You ignored that slow, flowing river.

Ignored the strength of the rays on your shoulders,
only concerned with impression

and expression,

of a soul that was to become You.

They said....

I hadn't thought,
not considered.
Until the bird appeared at my side
and I recalled you were a like a sparrow,

they said.

Our nest was full I guess
and your egg had been broken,
raided by me,
in our rushed wisdom.

I still think of you
through crushed tears.
On reminded days of
almost school books,
and candles in drawers.

If Someone...

If someone were to ask why I love you
I would reply I could not say
Love is not only blind to those

that agree its terms
It cushions you to the blow of reason
I could say it is your hair
the way it frames a perfect face
I could site your eyes as being windows
into a mind I can never understand
I may even be as brash

as to describe the incredible

innocence of your shoulders
that form on an early morning,
a sculpture so pure.
If someone were to ask me

why I stay with you
when words appear as harshly

as an unforeseen thunderstorm
I would say it is written somewhere
that a spark creates a burning fire.
And a flame is preferable to me,
In this short life
and while all around me fools talk of love
mine will remain unspoken
because the soul never speaks
It is left just to wonder,
at the beauty of it all.

The End

It feels like the end he said.
Or the start of it. With these aches and pains.
Leading me and reminding me
That cures don't waste their time.
On fools like me anymore.

And friends are checking out
Leaving unpaid bills.
And incomplete.
Sudden memories.
Elbowing their way to the front of minds.

Here I am hanging on
To another decade or two.
Still collecting souvenirs.
Realising that nothing is ever anyones.
Only a feint stench of shame.

Was this a life lived?
A wallpaper life. Interspersed.
With cigarettes. To break monotony.
With drink. To overcome the senses.

With morphine to welcome in the hell.

Printed in Great Britain
by Amazon

26496670R00046